Luke's ⌐

Written by Chris Lutrario
Illustrated by John Hurford

Collins Educational

An Imprint of HarperCollins*Publishers*

Luke did not want to
hang up his coat.

Luke did not want his mum to go.

Luke did not want to
sit on the carpet.

Luke did not want to
go into the big hall.

Luke did not want to go out into the playground.

But when his teacher
said, "Who wants to
play with the sand?"

Luke said, "Me!"